Trees

Todd Telander

FALCONGUIDES ®

GUILFORD, CONNECTICUT
HELENA, MONTANA
AN IMPRINT OF GLOBE PEQUOT PRESS

To my wife, Kirsten, my children, Miles and Oliver, and my parents, all of whom have supported and encouraged me through the years.

To buy books in quantity for corporate use or incentives, call **(800) 962-0973** or e-mail **premiums@GlobePequot.com.**

MIX
Paper from responsible sources
FSC® C005010

FALCONGUIDES®

FalconGuides is an imprint of Globe Pequot Press.
Falcon, FalconGuides, and Outfit Your Mind are registered trademarks of Morris Book Publishing, LLC.

Illustrations by Todd Telander
Text design: Sheryl P. Kober
Project editor: Lauren Brancato
Layout: Joanna Beyer

Library of Congress Cataloging-in-Publication data is available on file.

ISBN 978-0-7627-7958-1

Printed in the United States of America

10 9 8 7 6 5 4 3 2 1

Contents

Introduction

The study of trees is a fascinating undertaking that can provide a lifetime of discovery. In addition to their attractiveness as individuals or entire forests, trees provide an essential role in the ecosystem by providing habitat and food for wildlife, stabilizing and enriching soils, and maintaining a stable atmosphere through photosynthesis. A tree is usually defined as a plant that produces woody growth, normally has a single trunk, and attains a height of at least 20 feet. Within this description fits an incredible array of forms, from the towering Redwood to the majestic, spreading Live Oak to the stunted and gnarled 4,000-year-old Bristlecone Pine. Although there are nearly 1,000 species of trees in North America, this guide is intended to serve as an introduction and overview of ninety of the more common trees in the United States and Canada. I have included representatives from most tree families, and focused on trees that are native to North America (although some introduced species are included if they have become naturalized).

Notes about the Entries

Order
This guide begins with the conifers, usually evergreen trees bearing needles and cones; moves to groups of trees such as the cactus, yucca, and palms; and finishes with the largest group, the broadleaf trees, normally deciduous, having hard wood and bearing seeds in some kind of fruit.

Names
Both common names and scientific names are included for the entries. Common names are better recognized, but they tend to vary regionally, and there may be more than one common name for each species. Less well known, the universally accepted scientific name of genus and species (such as *Populus deltoides* for Eastern Cottonwood) provides more reliable identification. Also, one can often learn interesting facts about a plant from the English translation of its Latin name. For instance, the generic name, *Populus,* is Latin for a kind of poplar tree, and *deltoides* means triangular, describing the overall triangular shape of the leaves.

Families
Trees are grouped into families based on similar structures, growth habits, and common ancestry. Once you are familiar with some of the more common families and their shared characteristics, you can often place an unfamiliar tree into a family, which will reduce your search to a smaller group. For example, if you find a broadleaf tree with palmately lobed leaves that grow opposite on branches and produce paired, winged fruits, you might first look in the family Aceraceae (which includes the maples) and narrow your search from there. You may find a diagram for leaf shapes, margins, and terms in the following chapter, Plant Terms.

Size
The size given for each tree is the maximum height and trunk diameter you are likely to find when environmental conditions are ideal and you are looking at a fully mature specimen. If conditions are less favorable, or if you find a specimen early in its growth

cycle, the tree may be much smaller. On the other hand, there are many examples of "champion" trees that have grown to sizes far larger than the norm.

Range/Habitat

The range of each species can be very wide, such as across the entire United States, or limited to a certain region, such as the Southwest or Northeast. Within a plant's range, it is important to note the specific habitat where it occurs, which can be an excellent key to identification. Although some nonnative, invasive trees grow almost anywhere, most have fairly specific environments where they prosper. Factors such as soil conditions, temperature, water availability, elevation, and surrounding vegetation all play an important role in a tree's ability to survive. You won't find Baldcypress growing in the desert or Joshua Trees growing in swamps. Plants used as ornamentals are an exception, often being found far from their natural habitat.

Descriptions

The descriptions give the essential information needed for identification: the basic shape and character of the tree and characteristics of leaves, branches, bark, flowers, and fruits. Other clues may sometimes be included: hairiness (or lack of hairs), spines, textures, and odors. The identity of unique plants may be obvious, whereas others are so similar that they may require the use of additional references or a key to ensure proper identification.

Illustrations

The illustrations are designed to help in identification by showing the most important structures. They may include a simple profile of the mature tree, a representative leaf, the texture of the bark, and a fruit or flower. Keep in mind that these parts can show extreme variability; the illustrations represent averages and are not intended to be used alone, but rather to supplement information provided by the text.

Plant Terms

For the most part, I have chosen to use common terms to describe the trees, although botanists have developed an elaborate language of their own. A few of the scientific terms that I have included in the text have to do with flower parts, leaf shape, leaf margins, and leaf arrangement, and are illustrated here.

Flower Parts

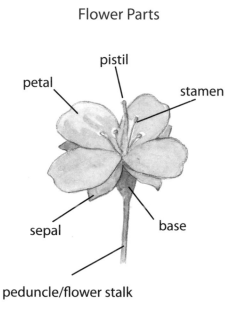

pistil

petal

stamen

sepal

base

peduncle/flower stalk

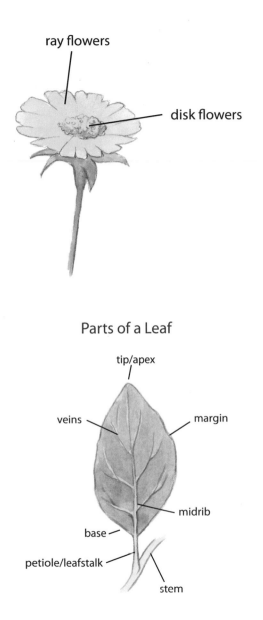

ray flowers

disk flowers

Parts of a Leaf

tip/apex

veins

margin

midrib

base

petiole/leafstalk

stem

Common Leaf Shapes

| ovate | elliptical | lanceolate | cordate | spatulate | linear |

Leaf Margins

entire/
smooth serrate/
toothed crenate incised lobed pinnately
divided palmately
divided

Leaf Arrangement

alternate   opposite   whorled

Baldcypress, *Taxodium distichum*
Cypress family (Cupressaceae)
Alternate name(s): Swamp Cypress
Size: Up to 120' tall, diameter to 5'
Range/habitat: Swamps and flooded lowlands of the deep South and along the Mississippi Valley

Description: A relic from a lineage of prehistoric trees, the Bald-cypress is a large, deciduous conifer with a wide, buttressed lower trunk (often submerged), stout upper trunk, and well-branched limbs giving a rounded crown. The foliage is often laden with drooping clumps of Spanish moss. A peculiar aspect is the presence of knobby, conical, woody "knees" that arise some distance from the trunk. The bark is gray or brown and broken into long, longitudinal, fibrous ridges. The leaves are flat needles, to .75 inch long, arranged in two ranks along the branches. Unlike most conifers, this species loses its leaves, still attached to their branchlets (the small, terminal branches), each autumn. The fruit is a small (to 1 inch wide), grayish, ball-like cone with fused scales. Baldcypress is renowned for the incredible durability of its wood.

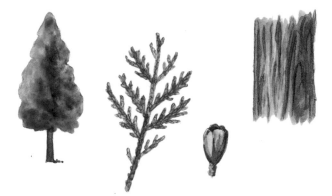

Northern White Cedar, *Thuja occidentalis*
Cypress family (Cupressaceae)
Alternate name(s): Eastern Arborvitae
Size: Up to 60' tall, diameter to 3'
Range/habitat: Wet coniferous forests and swamps of northeastern United States and southeastern Canada

Description: The Northern White Cedar is a medium-size, evergreen conifer with a relatively narrow, conical profile and dense foliage. It is one of the longest-lived trees of eastern North America. The branches terminate with branchlets that are entirely composed of small, dark-green, flattened, overlapping scales. Each spray of branches is fanlike and flattened overall. When crushed, the leaves release their familiar, pleasant cedar scent. The bark is deep reddish brown, becoming grayish with age, with shallow furrows and somewhat fibrous peeling ridges. The fruit is a small, fleshy cone (called a "strobile"), up to .5 inch long, oblong, and composed of several overlapping scales. It grows in clumps along branchlets. The Northern White Cedar can reproduce from branches that come in contact with the ground, and it is often grown out of range as a small, shrubby, ornamental tree. It is closely related and anatomically similar to the larger Western Red Cedar of the northwestern United States.

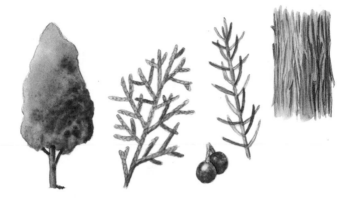

Eastern Redcedar, *Juniperus virginiana*
Cypress family (Cupressaceae)
Alternate name(s): Red Juniper, Pencil Cedar
Size: Up to 50' tall, diameter to 2'
Range/habitat: Open, dry soils; rocky areas; and hillsides of eastern United States

Description: The Eastern Redcedar is a medium-size, evergreen conifer with dense foliage and a compact, conical to narrowly rounded crown. It is not a true cedar, but more aptly called a juniper. It produces two kinds of leaves: The predominant type is found as tiny, green, overlapping scales that form fanlike branchlets that are round in cross section. The other type, found in young trees and new growth of older trees, is needlelike (to .5 inch long) and sharp, growing all around the branches. The bark is reddish brown or pinkish, with thin, longitudinal, shredding ridges. The fruit is a small, round, berrylike fleshy cone, about .25 inch wide, colored dark purple with a whitish bloom. Eastern Redcedars are often grown as ornamentals or for shelterbelts, and the berries are relished by wildlife.

Redwood, *Sequoia sempervirens*
Cypress family (Cupressaceae)
Alternate name(s): Coast Redwood
Size: Up to 300' tall or more, diameter 6 to 12'
Range/habitat: Moist, coastal fog belts of California and southern Oregon

Description: The Redwood is the world's tallest tree, with a record height of 379 feet, and among the longest living, with specimens over 2,000 years old. It is an evergreen conifer with a straight, massive trunk and a sparse, roughly conical crown of slightly drooping branches. The most predominant leaves are flattened needles (to 1 inch long) with two light stripes beneath, growing in ranks of two rows along branches. On new twigs and on the stalks of cones, there are shorter, scalelike leaves that grow all around the branch. Needles do not drop individually but in short sprays. The bark is rough and fibrous, reddish in color, deeply furrowed, and often marked with scars and charred areas. The cones are brown, small (to 1 inch long), ovoid, and hang singly from stalks. Redwoods also reproduce by shoots arising from the stumps of felled trees.

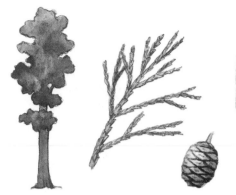

Giant Sequoia, *Sequoiadendron gigantea*
Cypress family (Cupressaceae)
Alternate name(s): Sierra Redwood
Size: Up to 300' tall, diameter up to 25'
Range/habitat: Mid- to high-elevation mineral soils in scattered groves along the western Sierra Nevada Mountains of California

Description: The Giant Sequoia is a massive, long-lived, evergreen conifer with a very wide, buttressed trunk and a sparse, irregular, somewhat columnar crown, often with bare larger branches on older trees. It is the world's largest tree by mass, and has the widest trunk (over 35 feet in one specimen). The leaves are slender and pointed, to .25 inch long, and arranged as overlapping scales on branchlets. Tightly packed on older growth, they are looser and spreading on new shoots. The bark is very thick, fibrous, reddish brown, with deep, longitudinal furrows and ridges. The base of some trunks becomes hard and burled, and may be split or charred from fire. The cones are egg shaped, about 2.5 inches long, brown, and composed of tightly packed, woody scales. They remain on the tree for many years before they open from the heat of fire or very dry, hot weather.

Sugar Pine, *Pinus lambertiana*
Pine family (Pinaceae)
Alternate name(s): Big Pine
Size: Up to 200' tall, diameter to 6'
Range/habitat: Mountainous, mid- to high-elevation slopes of California and Oregon

Description: The world's tallest pine, the Sugar Pine is a massive, evergreen conifer with a thick trunk, pyramidal crown, and irregularly spaced branches. It usually grows in mixed stands with other conifers. The needles are grouped in bunches of five with a common basal sheath, are about 3 inches long, and twisted along the axis. They are blue green above and grayish below with pale stripes. The brownish-to-gray, scaled bark becomes deeply fissured with age, and contains a sugary resin (hence the common name). The cones are very long (up to 2 inches), narrowly cylindrical, and have a long stalk. Their scales are smooth, orange brown, and somewhat shiny, with no prickles at their tips.

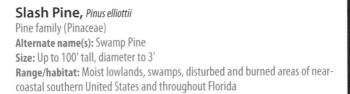

Slash Pine, *Pinus elliottii*
Pine family (Pinaceae)
Alternate name(s): Swamp Pine
Size: Up to 100' tall, diameter to 3'
Range/habitat: Moist lowlands, swamps, disturbed and burned areas of near-coastal southern United States and throughout Florida

Description: The Slash Pine is a medium-size, evergreen conifer with a tall, branchless trunk and a high, rounded crown. The term "slash" refers to its boggy, scrubby habitat. The dark green needles are borne in clumps of two (sometimes three) and joined at the base with a sheath. They are quite long (up to 11 inches), rigid, and grow in tufts that are concentrated at the end of branches. The bark is scaly, gray to orange brown, breaking and peeling in large flakes in older trees. The cones are glossy dark brown, egg shaped, to 6 inches long, and short-stalked. The scales end with a short, curved prickle.

Loblolly Pine, *Pinus taeda*
Pine family (Pinaceae)
Alternate name(s): Oldfield Pine
Size: Up to 100' tall, diameter to 3'
Range/habitat: Open flatlands, swamps, sandy soils to 2,000' in southeastern United States

Description: The Loblolly Pine is an evergreen conifer with a straight trunk and a high, broad crown. It is the tallest pine of the Southeast. The needles are long (to 9 inches), yellowish green, have pointed tips, and are sometimes twisted. They grow in bundles of three (sometimes two), and are mostly concentrated in dense tufts at the ends of branches. The bark is reddish brown and broken into thick, irregular plates. The cones are stalkless, to 5 inches long, egg shaped to conical, and reddish brown. Each scale is tipped with a prickly spine. The term "loblolly" refers to swampy lowlands, although this species thrives in a wide variety of soils.

Lodgepole Pine, *Pinus contorta*
Pine family (Pinaceae)
Alternate name(s): Tamarack Pine, Shore Pine
Size: Up to 90' tall, diameter to 3'
Range/habitat: Mountainous and coastal areas of western United States to 11,000'

Description: The Lodgepole Pine is an evergreen conifer that takes a wide variety of forms. It is straight and erect with a sparse, narrow crown in mid- to high-elevation mountain forests (giving the tree its common name), but short and stubby with a contorted trunk in windswept coastal areas. The needles are two to a bundle, joined at the base with a sheath, are 1 to 3 inches long, dark green, and pointed at the tip. The bark is gray to brownish, thin, and broken into small, round-edged scales. Coastal trees may have nearly black bark. The smallish cones are light brown, egg shaped, up to 2 inches long, and often flattened on one side. The tip of each scale has a small prickle. The heat of fire is usually required to release the seeds of the cone for successful propagation.

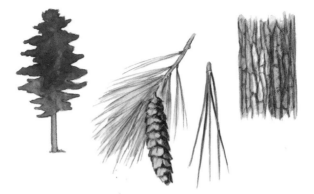

Eastern White Pine, *Pinus strobus*

Pine family (Pinaceae)
Alternate name(s): Weymouth Pine
Size: Up to 120' tall, diameter to 4'
Range/habitat: Wet, cool forests of northeastern United States to 4,500'

Description: The tallest tree in the eastern United States, the Eastern White Pine is a majestic, evergreen conifer with stout, sparse branches and a conical profile. In older trees the lower branches are lost and the crown becomes broadened. The needles are long and thin, to 5 inches long, and bunched into groups of five with a short sheath at the base (the only eastern pine with five needles to a bunch). They are bluish green above and pale gray green below. The bark is gray or gray brown and broken into scaly, interlocking plates that become more pronounced in older trees. The cone is narrow and long (to 8 inches long), sometimes curved, with widely spaced scales without prickles. Mature cones have a short stalk and hang pendant on branches.

Pitch Pine, *Pinus rigida*
Pine family (Pinaceae)
Size: Up to 55' tall, diameter to 2'
Range/habitat: Rocky slopes to moist coastal soils of the Appalachians and northeastern United States

Description: The Pitch Pine is a small, evergreen conifer with a stout trunk and a rounded to broad, irregular crown. It may reproduce by suckers from the trunk base, forming multiple, gnarled stems. The needles are thick and rigid, sometimes twisted, up to 5 inches long, and grow in clumps of three with a basal sheath. The bark is reddish brown to gray, broken into irregular, scaly plates, sometimes with blisters of protruding pitch. The cones are about 2.5 inches long, egg shaped, yellowish brown, and borne in groups of two (sometimes three). The scales are tipped with a sharp prickle. Some cones will remain on the tree until broken apart by fire. The Pitch Pine is named for its particularly resinous wood.

PINE FAMILY

Bristlecone Pine, *Pinus longaeva*
Pine family (Pinaceae)
Alternate name(s): Great Basin Bristlecone Pine
Size: Up to 50' tall, diameter to 5'
Range/habitat: High-elevation (near tree line), arid mountain slopes of the Great Basin region

Description: The Bristlecone Pine is an evergreen, coniferous tree with a thick, short trunk and relatively sparse, irregular crown. Extremely long-lived, specimens more than 4,000 years old make it the oldest known nonclonal life form. These old trees are highly gnarled, disfigured, and contain large remnants of dead wood. The needles are around 1 inch long, grow in clumps of five, and encircle the branch like a bottle brush or fox's tail (Bristlecone Pines are closely related to Foxtail Pines). The bark is reddish brown to gray, scaly, and broken into plates. With age, much bark is missing, leaving only weathered, bare, twisted wood. The cones are broadly oval, about 3 inches long, colored purple when young and becoming reddish brown at maturity. The thick scales are tipped with long, inward-curving prickles.

Whitebark Pine, *Pinus albicaulis*
Pine family (Pinaceae)
Alternate name(s): Pitch Pine, Scrub Pine, White Pine
Size: Up to 60' tall, diameter to 2'
Range/habitat: High elevations to timberline near 12,000' in the northern Rocky Mountains, Cascades, and Sierra Nevada Mountains

Description: The Whitebark Pine is a short, long-lived, evergreen conifer of high altitudes. On lower slopes, it grows much like a traditional conifer, but on the higher, windswept, rocky ridges it will take on a disfigured, stunted, "krumholtz" shape with a gnarled trunk and crooked branches. The needles are about 2 inches long, light green, stiff but flexible, and grow in bundles of five. They mostly occur in clumped tufts at the ends of branches. The bark is light gray with variable amounts of darker spotting and scaling, and often twisted or burled in exposed, older trees. The cones are egg shaped, to 3 inches long, colored dark violet brown to blackish, with compact, blunt scales that have a pale tip. The seeds of the cone are a favored food for the Clark's nutcracker, which is instrumental in dispersing them. Whitebark Pine populations have suffered greatly from damage due to beetles and fungal disease.

Ponderosa Pine, *Pinus ponderosa*

Pine family (Pinaceae)
Alternate name(s): Western Yellow Pine, Blackjack Pine
Size: Up to 180' tall, diameter to 5' (Pacific forms largest)
Range/habitat: Moist to dry regions and mountain slopes to 10,000' in the western United States

Description: The Ponderosa Pine is a tall, robust, evergreen coni-fer with a broad crown, open canopy, and an often-bare lower trunk. It commonly forms parklike stands. The needles are dark green, quite long (5 to 10 inches), and arranged in clumps of three (sometimes two or five) with a basal sheath. They form conspicu-ous rounded tufts at the end of branches. The bark is blackish to dark red when young, becoming golden pink to light red upon maturity, and is broken into jigsaw-puzzle-like plates delineated by blackish furrows. The twigs, when broken, emit a resinous cit-rus odor. The cones are stout, ovoid, 3 to 6 inches long, with thick scales that terminate in a sharp, inward-facing prickle, and hang below the branch. The Ponderosa is a very important tree in the timber industry, rivaling the Douglas-fir.

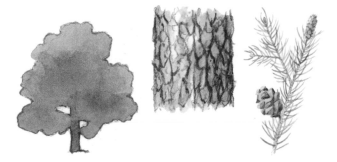

Pinyon Pine, *Pinus monophylla*

Pine family (Pinaceae)

Alternate name(s): One-leaf Pinyon Pine, Singleleaf Pinyon, Piñon Pine

Size: Up to 35' tall, diameter to 1.5'

Range/habitat: High desert, mesas, foothills of southwestern United States

Description: The Pinyon Pine is a relatively small, evergreen conifer with a rounded crown and a trunk that is usually branched close to the base. It is a slow-growing tree and can reach ages of 200 years or more. The bark is textured with scales, and the leaves are in the form of thin, curving needles up to 2 inches long that occur singly along the stem. Male, pollen-producing cones occur in clumps, whereas the female, seed-producing cones occur singly and are compact with tough scales. This cone takes two years to mature. A very similar species, *Pinus edulis,* has two clumped needles arising at the leaf base. The large pine nuts are delicious and high in fat and protein, and the wood makes fragrant firewood.

Douglas-fir, *Pseudotsuga menziesii*
Pine family (Pinaceae)
Alternate name(s): Douglas-spruce, Oregon Pine
Size: Up to 300' tall (coastal larger, Rocky Mountains smaller), diameter to 5'
Range/habitat: Western United States coastal or Rocky Mountain regions to 10,000'

Description: The Douglar-fir is an evergreen conifer whose coastal variety is the world's second-tallest tree after the Redwood. Its shape is somewhat conical with long, drooping branches, and it may form great stands. The needles, about 1 inch long, are dark green or bluish green (bright yellow in new growth), flat, growing singly along twigs, and soft-tipped. The foliage smells of citrus when crushed. Buds are reddish orange and pointed, and the bark is pale gray and relatively smooth when young, becoming darker reddish brown and fissured with age. The cone is light brown, up to 4 inches long, roughly oval shaped, with distinctive, three-pronged bracts that protrude above the scales. Cones hang like pendants and fall off intact, unlike the cones of true firs that grow erect and fall in pieces. The Douglas-fir is a very important tree in the timber industry due to its fast growth and very straight, uniform trunk that often lacks branches along its lower portion.

Noble Fir, *Abies procera*
Pine family (Pinaceae)
Alternate name(s): Red Fir, Larch
Size: Up to 150' tall, diameter to 4.5'
Range/habitat: Coastal mountains and Cascades of northwestern United States

Description: The tallest fir, the Noble Fir is an evergreen conifer with an arrow-straight, thick trunk, cylindrical profile, and crown that is domed, unlike the pointed crown of most firs. The needles are bluish green, to 1.5 inches long, rigid, with pointed tips. Older, lower branches have softer and flatter needles that splay out in flat sprays, while those of new, fertile growth are plump and curved upward at the tip, creating a dense mass on the upper surface of the branch. The bark is grayish and broken into numerous small, irregular plates. The cones are up to 7 inches long, cylindrical, and grow erect on the upper branches. The scales are hidden beneath a covering of golden greenish-brown, pointed, downward-curving bracts.

White Fir, *Abies concolor*
Pine family (Pinaceae)
Alternate name(s): White Balsam, Rocky Mountain White Fir
Size: Up to 150' tall, diameter to 3'
Range/habitat: Scattered mountainous regions across the western United States, especially on drier slopes

Description: The White Fir is a widespread, evergreen conifer with a typical fir shape: tall, spirelike crown and a particularly massive trunk. Its bluish green needles are about 2 inches long, flat, with a blunt or slightly pointed tip and undersides that show pale, longitudinal stripes. They are arranged in flattened sprays of two rows in older growth, but grow all around the upper surface of the branches in new growth. When plucked, the needles leave a round depression on the branch, and when crushed, they release a pleasant citrus aroma. The bark is smooth, grayish, with resinous lumps in young trees; it becomes thick and deeply furrowed with age. The cones are cylindrical, up to 5 inches long, greenish to purple brown, with closely packed scales. They grow erect on the upper branches, releasing scales while still attached, leaving the spindlelike core intact. A very similar species, the Sierra White Fir, grows predominantly in mountainous California.

Balsam Fir, *Abies balsamea*
Pine family (Pinaceae)
Alternate name(s): Canada Balsam Fir, Balm of Gilead
Size: Up to 60' tall, diameter to 1.5'
Range/habitat: Moist, cool forests of northeastern United States to 5,500'

Description: The Balsam Fir is an evergreen conifer with the classic fir spirelike, conical shape, although trees on windswept slopes may be stunted and contorted. The needles are about 1 inch long and arranged in two opposite rows, forming flat sprays, although on new growth they may encircle the branch. They are shiny, dark green above, pale below, and relatively blunt at the tip. When removed, the needle leaves a small crater in the branch. Crushed foliage is aromatic with a pleasant, piney, resinous odor. The gray bark is smooth when young and dotted with resin-filled lumps. With age it becomes roughened with scales. The cones grow only on the uppermost part of the tree and stand erect on the branches. They are purplish brown, up to 4 inches long, narrowly ovate to cylindrical, and have tightly packed scales. At maturity, the scales break off while the cone stays on the branch, leaving a narrow, upright spindle.

Colorado Blue Spruce, *Piceae pungens*
Pine family (Pinaceae)
Alternate name(s): Blue Spruce, Silver Spruce
Size: Up to 100' tall, diameter to 2.5'
Range/habitat: Mid- to high-elevation, moist slopes and streamsides of the central Rocky Mountain region

Description: The Colorado Blue Spruce is an evergreen conifer with a pyramidal or spirelike, dense crown. The needles are firm, four-sided, about 1 inch long, with sharp tips. They vary from pale gray to blue green, and arise singly on branchlets from a persistent, knobby base. The bark is gray to gray brown with irregular scales and furrows. The cones are cylindrical to narrowly egg shaped, up to 4 inches long (longer that those of the similar Engelmann Spruce), light reddish brown, with thin scales that have toothed margins. They hang pendant on branches, as is typical of spruces. The Colorado Blue Spruce is often grown as an ornamental for its handsome, symmetrical shape and light-colored foliage.

Engelmann Spruce, *Piceae engelmannii*

Pine family (Pinaceae)

Alternate name(s): Mountain Spruce

Size: Up to 130' tall, diameter to 3'

Range/habitat: Mid- to high-elevation slopes of mountainous western United States

Description: The Engelmann Spruce is an evergreen conifer with dense foliage, a spirelike to columnar crown, and a short trunk that branches nearly to ground level. At higher elevations it can become stunted and misshapen. The needles are thick, rigid, rarely more than 1 inch long, and roughly four-sided in cross section. They are bluish green, prickly at the tips, and arise singly and radially (like a bottle brush) on the branches. Leafless twigs are distinctly rough and knobby. The bark is very thin, purplish to chestnut in color, and flaking in rounded scales. Mature cones are light brown, up to 2.25 inches long, narrowly egg shaped or cylindrical, and hang pendulous on branches. The scales are thin and soft with wavy margins.

Black Spruce, *Piceae mariana*

Pine family (Pinaceae)

Alternate name(s): Swamp Spruce, Bog Spruce

Size: Up to 50' tall, diameter to 1.5'

Range/habitat: High latitudes of North America and into northeastern United States in moist forests to 4,500'

Description: The Black Spruce is an evergreen conifer with a typical spruce shape of a dense spire with lower branches down to nearly ground level. It is often stunted where it grows in bogs or at its extreme northern range. The needles are stiff and thick, short (to .75 inch long), roughly four-sided in cross section, and prickly to the touch. They grow singly and radially (like a bottle brush) along the branch and are colored pale bluish green. Bare twigs are rough with old needle bases ("pegs") and are finely hairy. The bark is thin, reddish to grayish brown, and moderately scaled. Cones are small (to 1.5 inches long), egg shaped, and colored dark purple when young but maturing to light brown. The scales are thin with wavy margins. Cones hang pendant on branches, usually in groups near the top of the tree, and remain even after the seeds have matured.

Tamarack, *Larix laricina*
Pine family (Pinaceae)
Alternate name(s): Eastern Larch, American Larch
Size: Up to 60' tall, diameter to 2'
Range/habitat: Wet soils and bogs of northeastern United States; high latitude forests or tundra edges of Canada and Alaska

Description: Larches, including the Tamarack, are unusual conifers in that they are deciduous, losing their needles in winter. The Tamarack is medium-size (or quite small at it northernmost range), with delicate, sparse foliage that creates an irregular, open, pyramidal crown. The needles are soft and thin, about 1 inch long, light green, and like a flattened triangle in cross section. They grow in tufts from knobby "spurs" that arise at intervals on the branches. On young shoots, needles arise singly, spiraling around the branch. The foliage turns golden yellow in autumn. The bark is thin, pinkish gray to reddish brown, and heavily scaled. The cones are small (to .75 inch long), shaped like squat eggs, and grow erect on branches. They are deep red and leathery when young, turn woody and brown when mature, and have broad, smooth scales that hide the shorter scale bracts within.

Western Larch, *Larix occidentalis*
Pine family (Pinaceae)
Alternate name(s): Western Tamarack
Size: Up to 150' tall, diameter to 4'
Range/habitat: Mountain slopes of the inland Pacific Northwest and northern Rocky Mountains

Description: The Western Larch is the tallest larch in North America, is a deciduous conifer (like the Tamarack), and has delicate, sparse grass-green foliage in an open, pyramidal crown. In autumn it turns bright golden yellow before losing its needles. The needles are soft and thin, about 1.5 inches long, light green, and like a flattened triangle in cross section. They grow in tufts from knobby spurs that arise at intervals on branches. On young shoots, needles arise singly, spiraling around the branch. The bark is reddish brown, thick and scaly, becoming deeply furrowed into plates with age. The cones are up to 1.5 inches long, ovoid to elliptical, and grow erect from spurs on the branches. At maturity they are purplish brown with broad, rounded scales, each of which is accompanied by a distinctive, thin, pointed bract that protrudes past the scale.

Western Hemlock, *Tsuga heterophylla*
Pine family (Pinaceae)
Alternate name(s): Pacific Hemlock, Alaska Pine
Size: Up to 120' tall, diameter to 4'
Range/habitat: Pacific Northwest into northern California; Rocky Mountains to 4,500' on cool, moist slopes

Description: The Western Hemlock is an evergreen conifer with a pyramidal crown with a drooping tip; lacy, thick foliage; and branches that sweep upwards on young trees and arch downward on older ones. It is similar to the Eastern Hemlock but grows to greater heights. The needles are flat, flexible, up to .75 inch long, rounded at the tips, and of equal width along their length. Their color is dark, shiny green above and paler below with two whitish stripes. They grow in flat sprays of two rows, with some variation to this pattern. The bark is brown to grayish with scales demarcated by fissures that become quite deep with age. The cones are ovoid, light reddish brown, to 1 inch long, and hang downward, singly, at the tips of branchlets. The scales are broadly rounded with slightly wavy margins. Western Hemlock is very shade tolerant and therefore able to thrive in dense forests.

Eastern Hemlock, *Tsuga canadensis*
Pine family (Pinaceae)
Alternate name(s): Canada Hemlock
Size: Up to 75' tall, diameter to 3'
Range/habitat: Northeastern United States, including the Great Lakes and Appalachians, in cool, moist areas and rocky slopes.

Description: The Eastern Hemlock is a graceful, evergreen conifer with a pyramidal shape, lacy foliage, and a distinctive, drooping crown tip. It branches nearly to the ground, but in close stands branches are absent for some distance up the trunk. The needles are flat, flexible, to .5 inch long, and rounded at the tip. They are shiny dark green above and paler with two whitish stripes below. They grow in flat sprays of two rows, somewhat like a feather, and the bare twigs are rough and bumpy. The bark is dark brown (sometimes tinged with purple), and becomes deeply furrowed and scaly with age. The cones are small, up to .75 inch long, ovate, light brown, and hang downward, singly, at the tips of branchlets. The scales have smooth, rounded margins. This tree is quite similar to the Western Hemlock but is generally much smaller.

Pacific Yew, *Taxus brevifolia*
Yew family (Taxaceae)
Alternate name(s): Western Yew
Size: Up to 40' tall, diameter to 2'
Range/habitat: Mountainous and coastal Pacific Northwest, including northern California and northern Rocky Mountains

Description: The Pacific Yew is a small, sometimes shrublike, evergreen conifer with a generally rounded crown and a broad canopy that reaches nearly to the ground. The needles are soft and flat, up to 1 inch long, pointed at the tips and colored dark, glossy green above, paler below. They arise spirally on branches but bend to appear like two ranks making flat sprays. The bark is thin, with scales of grayish bark peeling away to reveal the red to purplish inner bark. The fruit is a bare seed that is surrounded by a bright-red, globular, fleshy cup (called an "aril"). This berrylike structure is about .3 inch long and borne singly or in small groups along the branches.

Saguaro, *Carnegiea gigantea*
Cactus family (Cactaceae)
Alternate name(s): Giant Cactus
Size: Up to 45' tall, diameter to 2'
Range/habitat: Desert plains of extreme southwestern United States (mainly California and Arizona) to 4,500'

Description: The Saguaro is a huge, unmistakable, long-living member of the cactus family. The erect main stem branches into a few or several arms, well above the ground, that curve upward or bend at odd angles. The trunk and branches are grayish green and fluted longitudinally with ridges and furrows that contain clusters of pale spines at intervals. Saguaros have the ability to expand or contract depending on the supply of water. There are no leaves, but the entire plant's surface contains chlorophyll and acts as a "leaf" in photosynthesis. Flowers are large (about 3 inches wide), funnel shaped, with white petals that surround a golden array of pistils and stamens, and bloom for one night only at the apex of the stems. The fruit formed is a bright-red, fleshy berry that contains innumerable tiny, black seeds. The Saguaro is very important in the desert ecosystem, providing food and housing for birds, insects, and bats, as well as construction material and food for humans.

Cabbage Palmetto, *Sabal palmetto*
Palm family (Arecaceae)
Alternate name(s): Swamp Cabbage, Cabbage Palm
Size: Up to 50' tall, diameter to 1.5'
Range/habitat: Warm, humid, or coastal areas throughout most of Florida and coastal Carolinas

Description: The Cabbage Palmetto is a tall, stout palm with a very straight trunk of uniform thickness, topped with a rounded mass of compound, fanlike leaves. The leaf fronds, up to 7 feet long, have a central stalk that gives rise to numerous, whiplike, dark-green leaf segments that spread in a modified palmate fashion. The margins of the leaf segments are pale and frayed into thready fibers. The bark (or more precisely, a kind of rind) of the young tree and upper trunk of the mature tree is crisscrossed with the remnants of old leafstalk bases. With age, the lower part of the trunk becomes smooth and hard, and colored grayish brown. Flowers are tiny, white, and borne on very long, branching clusters. The fruits are small, blackish, round, and fleshy, and hang in long clusters. New growth of the Cabbage Palmetto arises from a large bud at the apex of the trunk, which has been likened to a cabbage. Removal of the bud, however, usually results in the death of the tree.

Joshua Tree, *Yucca brevifolia*
Agave family (Agavaceae)
Alternate name(s): Yucca Palm
Size: Up to 30' tall, diameter to 2'
Range/habitat: Mojave desert of California; desert sections of Nevada, Arizona, and New Mexico to 6,000'

Description: Among the strangest of trees, the Joshua Tree is a short and compact tree with a stout trunk and multiple, thick, irregular branches that terminate in clumps of daggerlike leaves like those of other yuccas. These leaves are stiff, narrow, sharply pointed, up to 12 inches long, with fine-toothed margins. They form densely packed tufts at the end of branches. The bark is composed of packed woody tissue and often includes the compressed remnants of leaves from previous years. It is dark brownish and heavily textured with furrows and plates. The flowers arise at the tip of leaf clusters in packed groups. They are roughly bell shaped, creamy or pale greenish, and up to 2.5 inches wide. The ensuing fruit is an oblong capsule with a pointed tip that is up to 4 inches long, faintly ridged, first colored green then dark brown, and filled with large, black seeds.

Bigleaf Maple, *Acer macrophyllum*
Maple family (Aceraceae)
Alternate name(s): Oregon Maple, Broadleaf Maple
Size: Up to 90' tall, diameter to 3'
Range/habitat: Coastal forests and riparian areas of coastal and inland California, Oregon, and Washington

Description: The Bigleaf Maple is a deciduous broadleaf tree with a short, sometimes burled trunk; massive, spreading branches; and an irregularly rounded crown. In autumn, the foliage becomes golden to orange. The leaves are huge (up to 12 inches long) and the largest of any maple. They are glossy, dark green above, paler below, and palmately divided into five deeply incised, pointed lobes. They appear opposite on branches and have a very long stalk (as long as the leaf). The bark is gray and smooth when young, becoming fissured into longitudinal plates and turning brownish with age. Drooping clusters of yellow flowers give rise to the familiar "samaras" or "keys" of the maple family. These fruits are paired seeds, each with a winglike, papery bract, that together form an inverted V. They are up to 1.5 inches long, and their bases (near the seeds) are covered with fine hairs.

Red Maple, *Acer rubrum*
Maple family (Aceraceae)
Alternate name(s): Swamp Maple, Scarlet Maple
Size: Up to 75' tall, diameter to 2'
Range/habitat: Throughout eastern United States in a wide variety of habitats, especially areas with moist soils

Description: The Red Maple is a deciduous broadleaf tree with a stout trunk, widely diverging branches, and a broad, rounded crown. All plant parts exhibit some degree of reddish color, which is most pronounced in the fall when the foliage turns a brilliant, scarlet red. The leaves are about 4 inches long, subtly divided into three or five pointed lobes, with coarsely toothed margins. They are deep green above, paler below, and occur opposite on branches with long, reddish leafstalks. The bark is gray and smooth on young trees, becoming a darker grayish brown and furrowed into small plates with age. Bright orange-red flowers emerge in late winter, becoming the typical maple fruit of paired wings, or "samaras." They are borne on long, thin stalks and consist of the seed with a winglike, papery bract. These are pale red, becoming brown at maturity. Red Maples are important in maple syrup production and are often planted as ornamentals.

Sugar Maple, *Acer saccharum*
Maple family (Aceraceae)
Alternate name(s): Rock Maple
Size: Up to 110' tall, diameter to 3'
Range/habitat: Midwestern and northeastern United States, often in cool shaded forests to 5,000'

Description: The Sugar Maple is a tall, statuesque, deciduous broad-leaf tree with a straight trunk and a lush, domed crown. In autumn, the foliage is a beautiful display of bright golden yellow, orange, and red. The leaves are about 5 inches long, palmately lobed into five parts with pointed tips and colored a muted green. They are borne on long leafstalks and arranged opposite on the branches. The bark is grayish and smooth when young, developing furrows and long, scaly plates with age. The fruit is the typical maple "samara," or "key"—a seed attached to a papery, winglike bract up to 1.5 inches long, that grows in pairs on long, thin stalks. The base of the samara is greenish, while the "wings" become light brown. The Sugar Maple is the main source of maple syrup, which is distilled from the sugary sap during winter months.

Vine Maple, *Acer circinatum*

Maple family (Aceraceae)

Alternate name(s): Mountain Maple, Oregon Vine Maple

Size: Up to 40' tall, diameter to 1'

Range/habitat: Shaded understory of large conifers, disturbed areas of coastal and near-coastal Pacific Northwest

Description: The Vine Maple is a small, deciduous broadleaf tree or large, thicket-forming shrub. It can have a single trunk or multiple thin trunks, and a low, sprawling canopy. The leaves are palmately divided into seven or nine (sometimes eleven) pointed, shallow lobes with coarsely serrated margins. They are pale green, often tinged with dull red, becoming brilliant orange to red in the autumn. They are arranged opposite on branches via long, thin leafstalks. The bark is relatively smooth, pale green to pinkish gray, with sparse striations and bumps. The fruit is the typical "samara" of maples, consisting of a rounded seed enveloped by a papery, winglike bract. These are borne in pairs, nearly 180 degrees opposite each other, and are orangey red maturing to pale brown. Vine Maples may propagate by means of lower branches coming in contact with the ground and forming new shoots.

Box Elder, *Acer negundo*
Maple family (Aceraceae)
Alternate name(s): Ashleaf Maple, Boxelder Maple
Size: Up to 75' tall, diameter to 3'
Range/habitat: Throughout the United States in open fields and along streamsides

Description: The Box Elder is a widespread, deciduous broadleaf tree with a short trunk that sometimes branches close to the ground as a shrub, and a wide, rounded crown. It is unique among maples in that the leaves are not simple, but pinnately compound. They have three to nine leaflets of about 3 inches long, which are broadly toothed or slightly lobed on short or absent stalks. The foliage is bright green, becoming yellow to orange in autumn. The bark is thick and rough, gray to brownish, developing deep furrows and ridges with age. The fruit is a "samara": a seed attached to an airfoil-shaped papery bract that grows in V-shaped pairs on thin stalks. Up to 2 inches long, the paired samaras are green to reddish, becoming brown, and found drooping in long clusters. Box Elders grow quickly and thus are commonly used as an ornamental or for windbreaks.

American Holly, *Ilex opaca*

Holly family (Aquifoliaceae)
Alternate name(s): Christmas Holly
Size: Up to 60' tall, diameter to 2'
Range/habitat: Coastal beaches, wet to well-drained soils of southeastern United States

Description: The American Holly is a small, evergreen broadleaf tree with a relatively thin trunk, many spreading branches, and a dense, narrow-to-broad pyramidal crown. At the northern part of its range, it may not be much more than a shrub. The leaves are thick, leathery, up to 4 inches long, and matte green above with pale yellow-green undersides. They are elliptic with a pointed tip and several sharp spines along the margin, and grow opposite on branches. The bark is grayish, fairly smooth, becoming roughened with small bumps with age. Tiny, pale-green-to-whitish flowers give rise to bright-red, round, fleshy drupes (often called "berries"), about .25 inch in diameter. They grow singly or in clusters on thin stalks. The American Holly is a popular ornamental tree often prized for Christmas decoration.

Paper Birch, *Betula papyrifera*
Birch family (Betulaceae)
Alternate name(s): Canoe Birch, White Birch, Silver Birch
Size: Up to 80' tall, diameter to 2'
Range/habitat: Across Canada and northern United States to 3,000' in cleared or burned areas or along streams

Description: The Paper Birch is a widely distributed, deciduous broadleaf tree with one trunk or a cluster of relatively narrow trunks and a rounded, open canopy. Arranged alternately on the branches, the leaves are ovate with pointed tips, 2 to 4 inches long, with sharp, doubly serrate margins. They are dark green above and paler below, turning yellow in autumn. The outer bark is creamy white with peeling, papery layers, and marked with dark, horizontal striations and oval marks. The inner bark is reddish, and older trees may show deep furrowing at the base. The fruit is an elongate, conelike structure called a "strobile," 1 to 2 inches long, which releases its seeds by disintegrating on the branch. The Paper Birch is often grown ornamentally. Native Americans used the bark to build canoes.

River Birch, *Betula nigra*
Birch family (Betulaceae)
Alternate name(s): Red Birch, Water Birch
Size: Up to 75' tall, diameter to 3'
Range/habitat: Wet bottomlands and streamsides throughout mid- and southeastern United States

Description: The River Birch is a relatively small, deciduous broadleaf tree with a short trunk that divides into spreading main branches, creating a broad, irregular crown. It may be shrublike with multiple trunks. The leaves are ovate with pointed tips, about 2 inches long, with doubly serrate margins and prominent veins. They are somewhat glossy green above, paler below, and grow alternately on branches with short leafstalks. The bark is pinkish to reddish gray, shredding into thin, ragged strips or scales. With age, the bark becomes hardened with furrows and platelike scales. The fruiting body is an oval, brown, conelike cluster of scaled seeds, about 1 inch long.

Red Alder, *Alnus rubra*

Birch family (Betulaceae)
Alternate name(s): Oregon Alder, Western Alder
Size: Up to 85' tall, diameter to 2'
Range/habitat: Low-elevation moist soils, coastal areas, streamsides of the Pacific Northwest and coastal California

Description: The tallest of alders, the Red Alder is a deciduous broadleaf tree with a narrow, tall trunk and a compact, domed crown. When growing in close stands, the trunk may be branchless for some distance above the ground. The leaves are oval to elliptic, about 4 inches long, with prominent venation, and doubly serrate margins that often curve under. They grow alternately on the branches. The bark is blotchy gray and whitish, sometimes rust colored where damaged, relatively smooth, but becoming scaly and bumpy in mature trees. Male flowers are borne in long, drooping catkins, about 5 inches long, while female flowers are borne in small (about .5 inch long) catkins that develop into hard, oval, dark brown, conelike structures called "strobiles" up to 1 inch long.

American Hazelnut, *Corylus americana*
Birch family (Betulaceae)
Alternate name(s): Filbert
Size: Up to 18' tall, diameter to 1'
Range/habitat: Mixed woodlands, streamsides, shady wet areas of eastern United States

Description: The American Hazelnut is a small, fast-growing, well-branched, deciduous broadleaf tree or large shrub that can prop-agate by underground rhizomes, so it often forms dense thickets. Its smaller branches and leafstalks are covered in stiff hairs. Leaves are roughly heart shaped, to 4 inches long, with pointed tips, and margins that are double serrate (have sets of small teeth between larger teeth). The leaves turn a beautiful reddish color in the autumn. Male flowers are yellow green and grow in droop-ing catkins, whereas the clusters of female flowers form an oval nut encased in an open-ended, tube-shaped, rough, ragged husk. The nuts and flowering stalks are an important food source for wildlife, and the dense growth of the Hazelnut provides shelter.

Flowering Dogwood, *Cornus florida*
Dogwood family (Cornaceae)
Alternate name(s): American Dogwood
Size: Up to 40' tall, diameter to 1.5'
Range/habitat: Native to eastern and southern United States in mixed hardwood forests; grown as an ornamental throughout the United States

Description: The Flowering Dogwood is a relatively small, deciduous broadleaf tree with wide-spreading branches forming a flat or broadly rounded crown. Its outer branches curve upwards at the tips. The leaves are variegated dark green above, paler below, oval or elliptical with pointed tips, and are 3 to 6 inches long. The venation is arching and parallel, and margins are smooth and wavy. The foliage turns bright red in autumn. The bark is dark brown, rough, and deeply broken into small, blocklike chunks. Dogwood is renowned for its showy white "flowers," which actually consist of a cluster of pale-green true flowers surrounded by four white bracts that have the appearance of petals. The fruit is a bright-red, oval, berrylike drupe that grows in clusters.

Black Tupelo, *Nyssa sylvatica*
Dogwood family (Cornaceae)
Alternate name(s): Black Gum, Sourgum
Size: Up to 90' tall, diameter to 3'
Range/habitat: Variety of habitats, from drier slopes to wet bottomlands throughout eastern United States

Description: The Black Tupelo is a small- to medium-size, deciduous broadleaf tree with a straight, unbranched trunk, rounded crown, and thin, horizontal branches. The base of the trunk may be swollen when growing in wet habitats. The leaves are elliptic to obovate with smooth margins; up to 5 inches long; and colored glossy green above, pale green below. They grow alternately on branches but sometimes form bunches near the tips of branchlets. The foliage becomes deep red in autumn. The bark is pale brown to grayish with narrow ridges and furrows, but with age breaks into distinct, blocky plates. The fruit is a small, roundish-to-oval drupe, about .5 inch long, that resembles a small olive. It is deep blue when mature; occurs in clumps of one to three on long, thin stalks; and contains a hard, ridged seed. Black Tupelo is sometimes considered part of a separate family, the tupelo family, or Nyssaceae.

Water Tupelo, *Nyssa aquatica*
Dogwood family (Cornaceae)
Alternate name(s): Swamp Tupelo, Cottongum, Water-gum
Size: Up to 90' tall, diameter to 4'
Range/habitat: Swamps with partial or permanent standing water along the coastal plains of southeastern United States and the Mississippi Valley

Description: The Water Tupelo is a deciduous broadleaf tree with a rounded crown. The lower trunk is grossly enlarged and buttressed (an adaptation to life in water), and tapers to a straight bole. The leaves, up to 12 inches long, are elliptic with pointed tips and smooth margins except for occasional large teeth. They are glossy green above, paler and hairy below, and release bits of down early in growth. In autumn the foliage is golden, reddish, and purple. The bark is thin, grayish, and scaly. The fruit is an oblong drupe, about 1 inch long, shaped like an elongated olive. It begins green, matures to dark purple, and contains a hard, ridged seed. Fruits grow in bunches on individual long stalks. Water Tupelo is an important tree for lumber and honey production. It is sometimes considered part of a separate family, the tupelo family, or Nyssaceae.

Common Persimmon, *Diospyros virginiana*
Ebony family (Ebenaceae)
Alternate name(s): American Persimmon, Eastern Persimmon, Simmon, Possomwood
Size: Up to 60' tall, diameter to 2'
Range/habitat: Middle and eastern United States in dry, open woodlands and fields

Description: The Common Persimmon is a deciduous broadleaf tree with a well-branched trunk, sometimes-drooping branches, and a rounded crown. Older bark is very dark (almost black) and cracked into rectangular blocks. The leaves are alternate, oval with pointed tips, and have a smooth margin. They are dark, shiny green above and paler below, with a short leafstalk. The flowers are divided between male and female. The more-conspicuous female (staminate) flowers are small, creamy white, fleshy, solitary, four-petaled, and shaped like little bells. The resulting edible fruit is borne on a short stalk, is round and fleshy, up to 2 inches wide, and colored orange with a pale bloom. The leaves turn a beautiful yellow orange to red in the autumn.

Russian-olive, *Elaeagnus angustifolia*
Oleaster family (Elaeagnaceae)
Alternate name(s): Oleaster, Wild Olive
Size: Up to 30' tall, diameter to 1.5'
Range/habitat: Scattered range throughout the United States in abandoned fields, poor soils, along streamsides

Description: The Russian-olive is a small, deciduous broadleaf tree introduced from Asia but now naturalized across the United States. It has a short trunk and spreading branches, giving a dense, irregularly rounded crown. It often takes the form of a large shrub with multiple stems, and may reproduce from suckers. The leaves are broadly to narrowly lanceolate, up to 4 inches long, with smooth margins. They are grayish green above, pale gray below, covered with silvery scales, and grow alternately on thorny branches. The bark is gray or brown, becoming nearly black, and covered by longitudinal, peeling strips. Small, yellow, fragrant flowers give rise to the olive-shaped fruits, about .5 inch long, that are pale yellow green. They are favored by wildlife, which helps to disperse the seeds. Russian-olive can be quite invasive and is considered a menace where it displaces native species.

Sourwood, *Oxydendrum arboreum*
Heath family (Ericaceae)
Alternate name(s): Lily-of-the-valley Tree
Size: Up to 60' tall, diameter to 1'
Range/habitat: Shaded, moist, and acidic soils of east-central and southeastern United States, especially along the Appalachian Mountains

Description: The Sourwood is a small, deciduous broadleaf tree with a thin, curving trunk, wide-spreading branches, and an irregular pyramidal crown. In many areas it is no more than a large shrub, having multiple stems. The leaves are simple, narrowly elliptic with pointed tips, about 6 inches long, with finely serrate margins. They are a lustrous yellow green above with paler undersides and turn scarlet red in the autumn before dropping. The bark is grayish brown, thick, and broken by deep furrows into blocklike plates and ridges. The flowers are white, shaped like upside-down urns, about .25 inch long, and hang in long rows. The resulting fruits are dry brown capsules that contain multiple small seeds. The Sourwood is popular as an ornamental and in the production of honey.

Pacific Madrone, *Arbutus menziesii*
Heath family (Ericaceae)
Alternate name(s): Coast Madrono, Madroña, Tree Arbutus
Size: Up to 90' tall, diameter to 3'
Range/habitat: Along the Pacific coast, especially on coastal mountain slopes; central Sierra Nevada; prefers drier slopes near oaks and redwoods

Description: The Pacific Madrone is an evergreen broadleaf tree (sometimes a large shrub), with a twisting, snakelike trunk, irregular lower branches, and an uneven, sometimes lopsided crown. The leaves are elliptic, about 5 inches long, with mostly smooth, wavy, often decurved margins. They are tough, waxy green above and pale below, and grow alternately, sometimes spirally so, on the reddish branches. They turn rusty orange before dropping. The bark is quite exquisite: The hard, silky-smooth inner bark (greenish, then red with age) is partly covered by paper-thin strips of peeling, reddish bark. In mature trees the inner bark is coated with irregular, permanent, curling scales. Clusters of tiny, white, bell-shaped flowers mature into bunches of coarse, fleshy, red-orange berries, each about .5 inch long.

Black Locust, *Robinia pseudoacacia*
Legume/Pea family (Fabaceae)
Alternate name(s): Yellow Locust
Size: Up to 75' tall, diameter to 3.5'
Range/habitat: Fields, disturbed areas of east-central United States and scattered areas across the country

Description: The Black Locust is a fast-growing, deciduous broad-leaf tree with widely spaced, crooked branches and an irregular, rounded, open crown. The trunk is often divided very close to the ground. The leaves are pinnately compound, with seven to nineteen oval, dull-green leaflets, each about 1.5 inches long, with smooth margins. They are arranged alternately on the branches, which themselves are lined with curved, sharp spines at the leaf bases. The bark is gray to pale reddish, rough, with deep furrows creating thick, corded, scaly ridges. The white, sweet-smelling, pealike flowers grow in long clusters. The resulting fruit is a long, narrow, flat pod, up to 4 inches long, green then turning dark brown, and containing several beanlike seeds. Black Locust is often planted outside its original range as a windbreak or to revegetate disturbed areas.

Eastern Redbud, *Cercis canadensis*
Legume/Pea family (Fabaceae)
Alternate name(s): Judas Tree
Size: Up to 45' tall, diameter to 1'
Range/habitat: Streamsides, moist bottomlands, shaded forest understory of eastern United States

Description: The Eastern Redbud is a small, deciduous broadleaf tree with a thin trunk, spreading branches, and a flattish, irregular crown. It may also take the form of a large shrub with multiple stems. The leaves are cordate (heart shaped), about 5 inches long, with short, pointed tips and smooth margins. They are colored soft green above, paler below, and turn yellow in the autumn. The bark is reddish brown with moderate fissures and scales, becoming furrowed with age. Before leaves appear, small, pink, pealike flowers cover the branches and twigs in a showy display. The fruits are thin, reddish-brown pods, about 3 inches long, that contain several dark-brown seeds. Eastern Redbud is often grown as an ornamental, and the flowers are edible.

Acacia, *Acacia greggii*
Legume/Pea family (Fabaceae)
Alternate name(s): Catclaw
Size: Up to 25' tall, diameter to 1'
Range/habitat: Arroyos and dry streambeds of deserts, arid woodlands, and scrub of southwestern United States

Description: Acacia is a small, deciduous broadleaf tree or well-branched shrub. Its branches are striking, lined at intervals with long, arching thorns that resemble a cat's claw, hence its alternate name. The leaves are twice pinnately compound, with small, oval or spatula-shaped, grayish-green leaflets. The bark is dark, rough, and deeply furrowed. The fragrant, tiny, pale-yellow or cream-colored flowers are borne on loose, cylindrical catkins and mature into large, reddish-brown pods, like peas, that contain the shiny, brown seeds. The pods often curve when dry and may remain on the plant throughout winter. Acacia provides important habitat for desert-dwelling animals, bees take the nectar to make excellent honey, and the pods are edible.

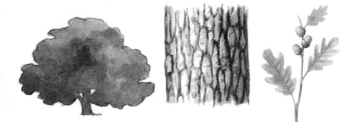

White Oak, *Quercus alba*
Beech family (Fagaceae)
Alternate name(s): Eastern White Oak
Size: Up to 80' tall, diameter to 3'
Range/habitat: A wide variety of habitats throughout eastern United States

Description: As a group, the oaks are long-living, deciduous broadleaf trees known for their choice hardwood and the production of acorns. The White Oak is a native to eastern North America with a wide canopy and thick, lateral limbs. The trunk can be quite massive, with grayish, cracked, or scaly bark. Leaves are alternate on the stems, somewhat oval or oblong, with several broad lobes and smooth margins. They undergo various color changes: first pinkish, then powdery gray, maturing yellow green, and attaining a reddish color in the autumn. The fruit is an acorn, which is relatively small (about 1 inch long), with a rounded tip, greenish brown, and held in a rough, woody cup. The edible (once cooked) acorns are high in protein and fat and are an important source of food for wildlife as well.

Southern Red Oak, *Quercus falcata*
Beech family (Fagaceae)
Alternate name(s): Spanish Oak
Size: Up to 85' tall, diameter to 3'
Range/habitat: Dry, upland, sandy soils from coastal New York to Texas

Description: The Southern Red Oak is a medium-size, deciduous broadleaf tree with a tall, straight trunk and a broad, rounded crown. The leaves are deeply lobed into three or five (sometimes seven) pointed sections with a thin bristle at the tip of each lobe. Arranged alternately on branches, they are deep, glossy green above, hairy and brownish below. The foliage is golden brown to reddish in the autumn. The bark is dark grayish brown, rough, and broken into scaly ridges. The fruit is an acorn, somewhat round (about .5 inch long), growing singly or in pairs. The lower, fat, scaly cup grows to about one third to one half of the way up the nut, which is green at first, becoming reddish brown at maturity, and having a short projection at its tip. The group of red oaks all have pointed, often prickled lobes on their leaves, and acorns that take two years to mature.

Northern Red Oak, *Quercus rubra*
Beech family (Fagaceae)
Alternate name(s): Red Oak
Size: Up to 80' tall, diameter to 3'
Range/habitat: Fertile soils, riparian areas of midwestern and eastern United States except in the far South

Description: The Northern Red Oak is a widespread, deciduous broadleaf tree that has a tall trunk and a high, rounded crown when growing in forest conditions, but may have a short, stout trunk and a low, broad crown when growing in the open. The leaves are simple, about 6 inches long, widest near their center, and cut into seven or more pointed lobes tipped with thin prickles. They are symmetrical, and the incised part of each lobe rarely reaches farther than halfway to the central rib. They are colored a deep, glossy green that becomes rusty orange to red in the autumn. The bark is dark gray, brown, or nearly black, rather smooth in young trees, but deeply furrowed with long ridges or plates in older trees. The fruit is an oblong acorn, about 1 inch long, with a narrow, scaly cup that covers only the base of the nut. The nuts are colored green when young, turn light brown when mature, and are found alone or in pairs on branches.

Southern Live Oak, *Quercus virginiana*
Beech family (Fagaceae)
Alternate name(s): Virginia Live Oak, Live Oak, Bay Live Oak
Size: Up to 50' tall, diameter to 4'
Range/habitat: A variety of low-elevation environments of coastal southeastern states from Texas to Virginia

Description: The Southern Live Oak is a statuesque, evergreen broadleaf tree with a short but massive, buttressed trunk, wide-spreading branches, and a crown that is typically wider than tall. The trunk and lower branches are often obscured by mosses. The leaves are elliptic or slightly ovate, about 4 inches long, generally with smooth, straight margins, but occasionally with a few spiked teeth. They are alternate on the branches, thick textured, and dark green above but paler and slightly hairy below. The bark is pale gray or grayish brown, deeply fissured, and broken into thick, blocky ridges. The fruits is an acorn, oval shaped, up to 1 inch long, beginning green and turning deep brown to blackish at maturity. The scaly cup at its base extends to about a third of the way up the nut.

Valley Oak, *Quercus lobata*
Beech family (Fagaceae)
Alternate name(s): California White Oak
Size: Up to 90' tall, diameter to 5'
Range/habitat: Valleys, foothills, and coastal areas of central and western California

Description: One of the largest broadleaf, deciduous trees of the western United States, the Valley Oak forms a dense, broad crown from a short, massive trunk that quickly divides into wide-spreading branches with smaller branches sometimes drooping to the ground. The leaves are oblong, widest near the tip, 2 to 4 inches long, smooth and dark green above with undersides paler in color and covered with fine hairs. They are deeply lobed with smooth margins and have yellowish veins. The foliage becomes yellow orange and brown in the fall. The bark is grayish to gray brown and is composed of thick plates broken by deep vertical and horizontal furrows. The fruit is an acorn, up to 2 inches long, with a bumpy, scaly cup encasing the long, pointed, smooth, golden-brown fruit. The acorns grow alone or in pairs.

Bur Oak, *Quercus macrocarpa*

Beech family (Fagaceae)

Alternate name(s): Blue Oak, Mossycup Oak

Size: Up to 75' tall, diameter to 3.5'

Range/habitat: Arid to moist lowlands of central United States, south to coastal Texas and north to Canada

Description: The Bur Oak is a deciduous broadleaf tree with a thick trunk (short when growing in the open; tall in dense stands), wide-spreading branches, and a rounded or domed crown. The leaves are obovate (widest near the tip), quite long (about 9 inches), and deeply incised, forming distinct upper and lower lobes. Growing alternately on the branches, they are glossy green above, paler green below, and become brownish yellow in autumn. Branchlets often have woody, lateral growths along their sides. The bark is grayish brown, scaly, and broken into irregular, longitudinal plates and ridges. The fruit is a fairly large (about 1.5 inches long), oval acorn with a deep, scaly cup rimmed with a fringe of dense hairs.

American Beech, *Fagus grandifolia*
Beech family (Fagaceae)
Alternate name(s): North American Beech
Size: Up to 90' tall, diameter to 3'
Range/habitat: Low- to mid-elevation moist soils throughout eastern United States

Description: The American Beech is a stately, deciduous broadleaf tree with a stout trunk, wide-spreading branches, and a dense, rounded crown. Suckers may grow from lateral roots, forming smaller trees at the perimeter. The leaves are elliptic to oblong, about 4 inches long, with pointed tips and widely spaced, coarse teeth along the margins. They are deep, shiny green above, paler below, and arise alternately on the stems with short leafstalks. The bark is slate gray and very smooth, even in older trees. Smaller branches grow in a zigzag pattern and contain thin, sharply pointed buds. The fruit is composed of an egg-shaped, reddish-brown husk about .6 inch long and lined with spines. Inside are two or three edible, teardrop-shaped nuts.

American Chestnut, *Castanea dentata*
Beech family (Fagaceae)
Size: Up to 30' tall, diameter to 1'
Range/habitat: Mixed woodlands of eastern United States, Appalachian Mountains

Description: The American Chestnut is a deciduous broadleaf tree whose original form has a wide, short trunk and a tall (to 100 feet), broad crown. The introduction of a fungal disease has eliminated most of these large trees, and what remains are short, shrubby versions that have grown from suckers of dead stumps. The leaves are elliptic to narrowly oblong, up to 8 inches long, bearing coarse spiny-tipped teeth along their margins. They are deep yellow green above, paler below, and grow alternately on branchlets via short leafstalks. The bark is grayish brown, initially smooth but fissuring into wide plates with age. The fruit is composed of a greenish-brown, rounded husk, about 2 inches wide, densely covered with long, rigid, branched spines. At maturity it splits into four parts to reveal two or three smooth, round, edible nuts.

Eastern Chinquapin, *Castanea pumila*

Beech family (Fagaceae)
Alternate name(s): Allegheny Chinquapin, Dwarf Chestnut
Size: Up to 30' tall, diameter to 1.5'
Range/habitat: Arid, sunny uplands on sandy soils of eastern and southern United States

Description: The Eastern Chinquapin is a small, deciduous broadleaf tree and a relative of the American Chestnut and often more of a bushy shrub in form. The trunk is well branched, with grayish, initially smooth, then furrowed bark. The leaves are alternate on the stems, up to 6 inches long, narrowly ovate to elliptic with pointed tips, and have spiny, serrate margins. Venation is fairly straight and crisp, and leaves are shiny green above with fine white hairs on their undersides. Male flowers are yellow and borne in long spikes, whereas the female flowers form a bristly, spherical husk (about 1 inch long) that is similar to but smaller than a chestnut and contains a single, smooth, edible, brownish nut.

Ohio Buckeye, *Aesculus glabra*
Horse-chestnut family (Hippocastanaceae)
Alternate name(s): American Buckeye, American Horse-chestnut, Fetid Buckeye
Size: Up to 50' tall, diameter to 2'
Range/habitat: Streamsides and moist fields of east-central United States

Description: The Ohio Buckeye is a relatively small, deciduous broad-leaf tree with a rounded crown and canopy that nearly reaches the ground. The trunk may be divided at ground level. The leaves are palmately compound, opposite on branches, with five or more leaflets radiating out from a central point on a long leafstalk. Leaflets are elliptic with pointed tips, about 4 inches long, with finely serrate margins. The foliage emits a disagreeable odor and turns yellow orange in the autumn. The bark is grayish with shallow fissures or tightly packed scales. The flowers, borne in dense clusters, are small, yellow, and bell-shaped with stamens longer than the petals. The resulting fruit is a brown, rounded capsule, about 1.5 inches long, and covered with distinctive, short, bumpy spines. The hard, dark, shiny seed inside has a pale circular area on one side, giving the appearance of an "eye."

Black Walnut, *Juglans nigra*
Walnut family (Juglandaceae)
Alternate name(s): Eastern Black Walnut
Size: Up to 100' tall, diameter to 4'
Range/habitat: Moist, rich soils and along streamsides in central and eastern United States

Description: The Black Walnut is a fairly large, deciduous broadleaf tree with a straight trunk and a rounded crown that becomes quite wide when growing in the open but is narrow with a long bole when cramped. Compound leaves (to 2 inches long) grow alternately on branches, and have many (usually fifteen to twenty-three) ovate, pointed leaflets with serrate margins. They are green and smooth above, paler with fine hairs below, emit a distinct musty odor, and turn yellowish in the autumn. The bark is dark gray or brown with a very rough, irregularly furrowed surface. The fruit is green, spherical, and tough (to 2 inches wide), and consists of a husk covering the meaty, edible nut within. It is borne singly, in pairs, or in groups of three. Walnut trees release chemicals that prevent the growth of surrounding vegetation, and a highly stain-ing dye is contained in the husk. The dark, fine-grained wood is prized by woodworkers.

Butternut, *Juglans cinerea*
Walnut family (Juglandaceae)
Alternate name(s): White Walnut
Size: Up to 60' tall, diameter to 2'
Range/habitat: Fertile, well-drained soils, streamsides, rocky slopes of the midwestern and eastern United States

Description: The Butternut is a deciduous broadleaf tree of similar stature to the Black Walnut but smaller, having stout limbs and an irregular, rounded crown. The compound leaves (to 28 inches long) are arranged alternately on the branches, and are pinnately divided into many (seven to seventeen) pointed leaflets with serrate margins. Pale yellowish green above, paler and hairy below, the leaves become golden brown in autumn. The bark is light gray, rough, with irregular cracks and ridges, but is smoother overall than that of the Walnut. The fruit is pale green, oblong, with subtle longitudinal ridges and a pointed tip, up to 2.5 inches long. The thick husk encloses a rough, oily, edible nut. The bark and husks have been extensively used to create an orange dye, and the wood is relatively light in color (hence the nickname of White Walnut).

Pecan, *Carya illinoinensis*
Walnut family (Juglandaceae)
Size: Up to 120' tall, diameter to 4'
Range/habitat: Lower-elevation fields, river valleys of south-central United States, particularly along the Mississippi Valley

Description: The Pecan is a tall, deciduous broadleaf tree with a straight, stout trunk; thick, spreading branches; and a rounded, irregular crown (that may be quite narrow in forested areas). It is the largest of the hickory trees. The leaves are pinnately compound, each with several (seven to nineteen) broadly lanceolate leaflets that curve at the pointed tips and have finely serrate margins. They are yellowish green above, paler below, and turn yellow in the autumn. The bark is gray to brown with moderate amounts of scales and fissures. The fruit is oblong with a pointed end, about 2 inches long, first green then rusty brown, and borne in clumps on very short stalks. The four-part outer husk separates at maturity to reveal a thin-shelled nut, which contains the edible and delicious seed.

Shagbark Hickory, *Carya ovata*
Walnut family (Juglandaceae)
Size: Up to 90' tall, diameter to 2'
Range/habitat: A wide variety of habitats, from woodlands to open fields to roadsides of eastern United States except for the far South

Description: The Shagbark Hickory is a deciduous broadleaf tree with a straight trunk and wide, rounded crown, tapering somewhat toward the bottom. The leaves are pinnately compound, composed of usually five elliptic or obovate leaflets about 6 inches long, with pointed tips and finely serrate margins. They grow alternately on the branches with a long leafstalk, and are colored grassy green above and pale green below. In autumn, the leaves are a spotty yellow brown. The bark, which gives the tree its name, is grayish and smooth when young, but in maturity peels into long, coarse strips that acutely curve out at their ends. The fruit is a round, ridged nut encased in a tough, fleshy, greenish-brown husk, about 2 inches wide, that splits into four parts. They often grow in pairs on very short stalks. The nuts are edible and delicious, and the wood is commonly used for smoking meats.

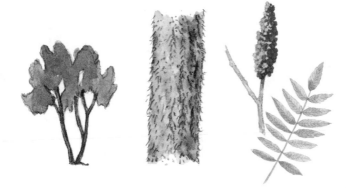

Staghorn Sumac, *Rhus typhina*
Cashew family (Anacardiaceae)
Size: Up to 30' tall, diameter to 9"
Range/habitat: Fields, disturbed areas, woodland edges of northeastern United States

Description: The Staghorn Sumac is a small, deciduous broadleaf tree or large shrub with sparse, thick branches that form a wide crown. The young, growing branches are coated with fine hairs, resembling the velvet of a stag's horn. The alternately arranged leaves grow up to 2 feet long and are pinnately divided into many lanceolate leaflets, about 3 inches long, with serrate margins. The leafstalks are densely hairy. The characteristic fruiting cluster is cone shaped and composed of many nonfleshy, hairy, deep rusty-red fruits. The leaves turn a beautiful red in autumn, and the clusters may remain attached to the plant throughout the winter. This plant propagates by seeds or underground rhizomes, and so often it will form closely spaced groups. The fruit cluster of Staghorn Sumac can be used to prepare a refreshing, lemonadelike beverage.

California Bay, *Unbellularia californica*
Laural family (Lauraceae)
Alternate name(s): Oregon Myrtle, Baytree, California Laural
Size: Up to 80' tall, diameter to 2.5'
Range/habitat: Coastal California and southern Oregon, often in the company of redwoods; slopes of the Sierra Nevada Mountains

Description: The California Bay is an evergreen broadleaf tree with a short trunk and a dense, broad, rounded crown which is often oblong in profile. Near the coast it may assume the stature of a stunted shrub. The leaves are lanceolate, tough, up to 5 inches long, with smooth margins. Arranged alternately on the branches, they are glossy green above and pale green beneath and release a distinctive peppery, camphorlike scent. The bark is grayish and smooth in young trees, but becomes dark brown and scaly with age, with thin peeling sections. The fruit (sometimes called a "California bay nut") is a firm, round, green drupe, about .75 inch long, that resembles an olive. These fruits grow singly on the branch via a short stalk and funnel-shaped base.

Sassafras, *Sassafras albidum*
Laural family (Lauraceae)
Alternate name(s): White Sassafras
Size: Up to 55' tall, diameter to 2.5'
Range/habitat: Fields, open woodlands, roadsides throughout eastern United States

Description: The Sassafras is a deciduous broadleaf tree with a broadly conical to well-rounded crown. The trunk may be straight and erect, thick and well-forked near the ground, or divided into several shrublike stems from suckers. The leaves are peculiar in that they may take three different forms: oval, mitten shaped with two uneven lobes, or trident shaped with three symmetrical lobes. They all are light yellowish green with smooth margins and become a pleasing yellow orange in the autumn. The bark in mature trees is gray to brown with deep fissures between rough, thick plates. Clusters of small, golden-yellow flowers mature into round, berrylike drupes, about .5 inch long, that are colored deep purplish blue. They are attached to brilliant-red, bulbous stalks. Besides being used as an ornamental, Sassafras is used commercially for its oil and as a tea.

Southern Magnolia, *Magnolia grandiflora*
Magnolia family (Magnoliaceae)
Alternate name(s): Evergreen Magnolia
Size: Up to 90' tall, diameter to 3'
Range/habitat: Low-elevation, swampy woodlands, streamsides of the coastal plains of southeastern United States

Description: The Southern Magnolia is a medium-size, evergreen broadleaf tree with a straight trunk and a rounded, often irregular crown and branches that may come nearly to ground level. The leaves are elliptic, up to 10 inches long, leathery, with smooth margins. They are dark, waxy green above and brownish with fine hairs below, and grow alternately on branches on short leafstalks. The bark is gray, relatively smooth except for shallow scales. The very large, showy, cream-colored flowers bloom throughout the summer. They are up to 10 inches across and are composed of several fleshy petals and sepals surrounding a central cluster of yellow pistils and stamens. Composed of overlapping scales, the fruit is conelike, oblong, about 3 inches long, and releases small, shiny, red seeds. The magnolias are among the more primitive of broadleaf trees and are popular as ornamentals.

Tuliptree, *Liriodendron tulipifera*
Magnolia family (Magnolicaceae)
Alternate name(s): Yellow Poplar, Tulip Poplar
Size: Up to 130' tall, diameter to 5'
Range/habitat: Deep, moist soils of eastern United States

Description: Among the tallest of eastern hardwoods, the Tuliptree is a deciduous broadleaf tree with a tall, straight trunk and a broadly columnar, rounded crown. The leaf shape is somewhat blocky, about 5 inches long, with four distinct lobes, smooth margins, and a long leafstalk. Some liken the shape to the profile of a tulip flower. They are colored deep, glossy green above and pale green below (becoming yellow in the autumn) and grow alternately on the branches. The bark is grayish brown, becoming deeply furrowed and ridged with age. The showy, solitary flowers are about 2 inches wide, yellow to greenish yellow, roughly tulip shaped, and have six petals. The fruit is a fleshy, cone-shaped structure of overlapping scales, which contains multiple seeds that are shed as the fruit matures. Fast growing and long-lived, the Tuliptree is important for lumber, honey production, and as an ornamental.

Red Mulberry, *Morus rubra*
Mulberry family (Moraceae)
Size: Up to 50' tall, diameter to 2'
Range/habitat: Low elevations throughout eastern United States in moist soils and riparian zones

Description: The Red Mulberry is a small, broadleaf deciduous tree with a short, thick trunk, wide-spreading branches, and a low, broad, rounded crown. The leaves are roughly oval in shape, about 5 inches long, and may be entire or deeply lobed into two or three parts. They are thin, have serrated margins, and are colored light green above and paler below with fine hairs. They appear alternately on the branches with a short leafstalk. Foliage turns yellow in the autumn. The bark is reddish gray and rough, breaking into thin, vertical scales with age. The edible fruits, about 1 inch long, are borne in tight, drooping clusters that resemble elongated blackberries. They begin green, maturing to red, then purple.

Osage-Orange, *Maclura pomifera*
Mulberry family (Moraceae)
Alternate name(s): Hedge-apple, Horse-apple, Bois d'arc
Size: Up to 50' tall, diameter to 2.5'
Range/habitat: A wide variety of soils in a scattered range throughout the United States

Description: The Osage-Orange is a small, deciduous broadleaf tree with a short trunk and a dense canopy of scraggly, rigid branches that form a broad, rounded crown, often to ground level. The leaves are ovate to broadly lanceolate, about 4 inches long, with pointed tips and smooth margins. They are alternate on the branches, and are light yellowish green above with paler undersides. Branches are normally laced with rigid, sharp spines up to 1 inch long. The bark is orangey brown with scaly, curving ridges and furrows. The fruit is a large, globular, greenish, softball-size mass composed of multiple, rounded sections. It is not edible, and it exudes a milky liquid when cut. The Osage-orange is unrelated to the true orange tree. It is native to the eastern Texas area but is now naturalized over much of the United States due to extensive planting as hedgerows.

Bluegum Eucalyptus, *Eucalyptus globulus*

Myrtle family (Myrtaceae)
Alternate name(s): Tasmanian Bluegum
Size: Up to 175' tall, diameter to 4'
Range/habitat: Scattered areas throughout California

Description: The Bluegum Eucalyptus is a very tall, evergreen broadleaf tree with a high, straight trunk and a relatively narrow, rounded crown, especially when growing in close stands. The mature leaves are lanceolate, up to 12 inches long, with pointed tips and smooth margins. They are tough, colored pale blue green, and have a strong menthol scent. They are arranged alternately on branches and droop on their short leafstalks. The bark is various shades of gray and composed of long, thin, peeling strips. The unusual flower is composed of a fuzzy cluster of whitish stamens emerging from a woody, stalkless, blue-green, cup-shaped capsule. The resulting fruit hardens, becomes bumpy, and ultimately splits, releasing small, black seeds. Eucalyptus is a native of Australia but has been naturalized and is sometimes invasive in California.

White Ash, *Fraxinus americana*
Olive family (Oleaceae)
Alternate name(s): American Ash
Size: Up to 110' tall, diameter to 3'
Range/habitat: Rich soils throughout the eastern United States

Description: The White Ash is a widespread, deciduous broadleaf tree with dense foliage, a stout, straight trunk, and a well-rounded crown. The leaves are pinnately divided into several (five to nine) elliptic, pointed leaflets, about 4 inches long, that have smooth or softly serrated margins. They are dark to yellowish green above, pale below, and each compound leaf is arranged opposite on the branches. The foliage becomes golden to purplish red in the fall. The bark is gray and fractured into narrow ridges and deep, elongated, diamond-shaped furrows. The fruit is a single samara, about 1.5 inches long, consisting of an oval seed at the base and a projecting, papery, paddle-shaped wing at the end. The samaras occur in large, drooping clusters. White Ash is popular as an ornamental and known for its use in baseball bats.

Oregon Ash, *Fraxinus latifolia*
Olive family (Oleaceae)
Size: Up to 75' tall, diameter to 3'
Range/habitat: Streamsides and moist soils to 5,000' in western Washington, Oregon, and California; also occurs in the Sierra Nevada foothills

Description: The Oregon Ash is the only ash common to the north-western United States. It is a medium-size, deciduous broadleaf tree with dense foliage, stout trunk, and irregularly rounded crown. The leaves are pinnately divided into several (five to nine) elliptic to oval leaflets, about 5 inches long, that have smooth or softly serrated margins. They are light green above with obvious pale veins, pale below, and each compound leaf is arranged opposite on the branches. The bark is gray to grayish brown and fractured into narrow, interlacing ridges and deep, elongated, diamond-shaped furrows. The fruit is a single samara, about 1.5 inches long, consisting of an oval seed at the base and a project-ing, papery, paddle-shaped wing at the end. They occur in large, drooping clusters. The Oregon Ash is popular as an ornamental and is also planted to control erosion.

Devilwood, *Osmanthus americanus*
Olive family (Oleaceae)
Alternate name(s): Wild Olive, American Olive
Size: Up to 40' tall, diameter to 1'
Range/habitat: Arid to moist areas along the coastal plains of southeastern United States

Description: Devilwood is a small, evergreen broadleaf tree or large shrub with lush foliage and a narrow trunk that divides close to the ground, forming a rounded crown. The leaves are narrowly elliptic, about 4 inches long, with smooth margins that curve under slightly. They are tough, glossy, dark green (paler below), and grow opposite on the branches. The bark is blotchy gray and relatively smooth except for small, wartlike bumps. The tiny, sweetly aromatic, off-white flowers grow in branching clusters. The fruit is a round or oblong olive (a kind of drupe or stone fruit), about .75 inch long, beginning green and maturing to deep blue. The common name, Devilwood, refers to the tough nature of the wood.

American Sycamore, *Plantanus occidentalis*

Sycamore family (Plantanaceae)
Alternate name(s): American Planetree, Buttonball
Size: Up to 100' tall, diameter to 8'
Range/habitat: Clearings, lowlands, streamsides of eastern United States

Description: One of America's most majestic trees, the American Sycamore is a massive, deciduous broadleaf tree with a thick trunk, wide-spreading, crooked branches, and a tall, broad, irregular crown. The leaves are yellowish green above, dull green below, usually as long as they are wide (from 4 to 9 inches), and palmately lobed into three or five lobes with jagged margins. They are arranged alternately on the branches. A distinctive aspect of the sycamore is its continually flaking bark that creates a patchwork of white, gray, and brown sections, often resembling the pieces of a jigsaw puzzle. The fruit is often called a "buttonball" and is more precisely a compact, globular, bristly, greenish-brown cluster, about 1.25 inches wide, that remains on the branches throughout the winter.

Carolina Buckthorn, *Frangula caroliniana* (aka *Rhamnus caroliniana*)
Buckthorn family (Rhamnaceae)
Alternate name(s): Indian Cherry
Size: Up to 35' tall, diameter to 1'
Range/habitat: Streamsides, rocky slopes of southeastern United States

Description: The Carolina Buckthorn is a small, deciduous broadleaf tree with a thin trunk and a rounded crown, often taking the form of a large shrub with several forking stems. The leaves are elliptic to obovate, about 4 inches long, with smooth or slightly toothed margins. They are dark glossy green above, paler below, and arranged alternately on the branches. The fall foliage is golden to reddish. The bark is gray to brownish, mostly smooth, with paler and darker spots in a horizontal pattern (like flattened ovals). The fruit is a small, spherical, fleshy drupe, about .5 inch across, that is initially red but becomes a dark blue purple at maturity. The fruits grow in clumps on short stalks.

Red Mangrove, *Rhizophora mangle*
Red Mangrove family (Rhizophoraceae)
Alternate name(s): American Mangrove
Size: Up to 35' tall, diameter varies
Range/habitat: Estuaries, brackish shorelines of coastal Florida and Texas

Description: The unmistakable Red Mangrove is a short, evergreen broadleaf tree with a widely branching, broad crown and a network of partially submerged, arching "prop" roots that anchor the tree into the silt and mud. The leaves are oval to elliptic with blunt tips, about 4 inches long, with smooth margins. They are fleshy, colored bright, dark green above and pale yellow green below, and grow opposite on branches. The bark is relatively smooth, brown to grayish, becoming scaled and furrowed with age. The flowers are dull greenish yellow, about 1 inch wide, and appear in sparse clusters. The resulting fruits are made of a bulbous, berry-like base from which emerges a slender, embryonic seedling up to 12 inches long. When released, these may float for months before anchoring in the soil to form new trees.

American Plum, *Prunus americana*
Rose family (Rosaceae)
Alternate name(s): Wild Plum
Size: Up to 25' tall, diameter to 1'
Range/habitat: Most of the United States east of the Rocky Mountains in rocky fields or near streamsides

Description: The American Plum is a small, often shrublike, deciduous broadleaf tree with a short, sometimes divided trunk and irregular, rounded canopy. The leaves are simple, ovate to elliptic with a pointed tip, up to 4 inches long, with finely double serrate margins. They are arranged alternately on branches with short leafstalks. The branches have intermittent, thorny spurs. The bark is smooth and brownish on younger trees, becoming rougher with age and splitting along the long axis into thin, curving scales. The whitish flowers have five petals, which is typical of members of the rose family. The resulting fruit resembles a commercial plum but is smaller (only 1 inch wide). Borne singly or in clumps on thin stalks, they are fleshy, orangey to purplish red, and contain a dark, flattened, hard pit.

Western Serviceberry, *Amelanchier alnifolia*
Rose family (Rosaceae)
Alternate name(s): Saskatoon Serviceberry, Alderleaf Serviceberry
Size: Up to 35' tall, diameter to 1'
Range/habitat: Arid foothills, higher elevations, disturbed areas of western United States

Description: The Western Serviceberry is a small, deciduous broad-leaf tree or large shrub with a fruit that ripens relatively early in the season. The leaves are alternate on branches, oval with rounded tips, about 1.5 inches long, and have finely serrate margins. The bark is pale gray, sometimes blotchy, and relatively smooth with shallow, vertical ridges and horizontal marks. Flowers are up to 1 inch wide, bloom early, have five thin white petals, and are borne loosely on spikes. The round berries are first greenish, then red, and finally a deep, dark purple. Berries can be harvested throughout the summer, and are an important food for wildlife and a favorite of bears.

Chokecherry, *Prunus virginiana*
Rose family (Rosaceae)
Size: Up to 25' tall, diameter to 1'
Range/habitat: Fields, streamsides, disturbed areas of central and northern United States

Description: The Chokecherry is a widespread, native, small, deciduous broadleaf tree or large shrub with thornless foliage. The leaves, about 3 inches long, are arranged alternately on the stems, have a thin petiole, are ovate with a pointed tip, and have finely serrate margins. They are colored glossy green above and pale green below. The bark is gray and mostly smooth except for small, raised, lenticular (lens-shaped) bumps. The flowers are white, five-petaled, and appear in tight clusters. The small, roundish berries are first red, then mature to a deep blackish purple, and occur in clumps as the flowers do. The berries are edible, and the longer they stay on the plant, the sweeter they will become.

Quaking Aspen, *Populus tremuloides*
Willow family (Salicaceae)
Alternate name(s): Trembling Aspen, Popple
Size: Up to 60' tall, diameter to 2'
Range/habitat: Northern and mountainous North America to 10,000', often in clearings from fire, and streamsides

Description: Named for the distinctive rustling of its foliage even in the lightest of breezes, the Quaking Aspen is a fairly small, short-lived, deciduous broadleaf tree and one of the most widespread trees in North America. It has a narrow trunk that supports a rounded or columnar open crown. The leaves are thick, rounded or cordate (heart-shaped), up to 3 inches long, with pointed tips and margins that are smoothly serrate. They are colored dark green above and pale green below. The leafstalk is long (as long as the leaf) and flattened. The foliage turns brilliant golden yellow in the autumn. The bark is smooth (not peeling), whitish or pale greenish, with horizontal striations and scattered dark, rough patches. The lower trunk can become very dark and heavily furrowed in older trees. The fruits are borne in long clusters (catkins) that release many downy-hairy–covered seeds. Aspens reproduce clonally by means of underground runners, hence are often found in thick groves.

Eastern Cottonwood, *Populus deltoides*
Willow family (Salicaceae)
Alternate name(s): Southern Cottonwood
Size: Up to 100' tall, diameter to 4'
Range/habitat: Prairies, lowlands, riparian areas throughout central and southern United States

Description: One of America's largest trees, the Eastern Cottonwood is a deciduous broadleaf tree with a thick, stout, sometimes buttressed trunk and upright branches that form a loose canopy with a broad crown. The leaves are triangular, 3 to 6 inches long, with pointed tips and serrate margins. They are glossy green and arranged alternately on branches with long leafstalks. The mature bark is gray with deep furrows and ridges, while that of younger trees is smoother and greenish. The fruits are small, green capsules borne in long, drooping clusters from which are released tiny seeds with tufts of fine, cottony hairs that allow them to float through the air.

Narrowleaf Cottonwood, *Populus angustifolia*

Willow family (Salicaceae)

Alternate name(s): Mountain Cottonwood, Willow-leaved Poplar

Size: Up to 60' tall, diameter to 1.5'

Range/habitat: Mid- to high-elevation riparian areas of the Rocky Mountains and Great Basin

Description: The Narrowleaf Cottonwood is a small, deciduous broadleaf tree with a thin, straight trunk; upright branches; and a narrow, irregular crown. It often grows in dense stands near stream banks. The leaves are lanceolate or narrowly oval with pointed tips (much like a willow leaf), about 3 inches long, with finely serrate margins. They grow alternately on branches and are colored grass green above, paler below, becoming golden yellow in the autumn. The buds are pointed and resinous. The bark is medium to dark gray or brownish gray, fairly smooth on young trees, but becoming rough with deep fissures and ridges with age. The tiny flowers are reddish and borne in drooping catkins; these become a clump of small, green capsules that release down-covered seeds. Narrowleaf Cottonwood is used as an ornamental or for erosion control due to its extensive root system.

Black Willow, *Salix nigra*
Willow family (Salicaceae)
Alternate name(s): Swamp Willow
Size: Up to 50' tall, diameter to 1.5'
Range/habitat: Moist soils, streamsides of eastern and southern United States; a variety of Black Willow grows in the Southwest and valleys of California

Description: One of the tallest of the willows, the Black Willow has one or a cluster of relatively thin, reclining trunks and a loose, rounded crown with drooping outer branches. The leaves are thin and lanceolate, 3 to 6 inches long, dark green above and pale below, with finely serrate margins. They grow alternately on the branches and have small stipules at the base of their leafstalks. The bark is dark brown to black (hence the common name) and broken into scaly ridges and furrows. Occurring in long clusters, the fruits are small, greenish, vase-shaped capsules with pointed tips that mature into seeds with cottony tufts of hairs.

American Basswood, *Tilia americana*
Linden family (Tiliaceae)
Alternate name(s): American Linden
Size: Up to 80' tall, diameter to 4'
Range/habitat: Throughout eastern United States in lower elevations with moist soils

Description: The American Basswood is a medium-size, deciduous broadleaf tree with a narrowly rounded crown and an overall symmetrical profile. Suckers from cut trunks may produce trees with multiple trunks. The leaves are cordate (heart-shaped) with thin, pointed tips, about 6 inches long, with an asymmetrical base (one lobe being lower than the other) and rough, serrate margins. They are dark green above, pale below (becoming dull yellow in the autumn), and grow alternately on the branches. The bark is brown to grayish, with neat, thin, vertical fissures. The sweet-smelling, yellow flowers, about .5 inch wide, are borne in drooping clusters that attach via their main stalk to a slender, leaflike bract. The fruit is a hard, round, brownish pea-size nut that remains attached to its long bract as it matures and falls from the tree. Basswood is often grown as an ornamental or shade tree and is valuable in honey production.

American Elm, *Ulmus Americana*
Elm family (Ulmaceae)
Alternate name(s): White Elm, River Elm, Soft Elm
Size: Up to 100' tall, diameter to 3'
Range/habitat: Mostly lower elevations in open areas or near rivers east of the Continental Divide

Description: The American Elm is a tall, stout, deciduous broadleaf tree with thick, vertically oriented lower branches that gracefully arch toward their tips, forming a broad, rounded crown. The foliage is limited to the upper portion of the tree, leaving a substantial bare lower trunk. The leaves are dark green, 3 to 6 inches long, elliptical, with a pointed tip. They are pinnately veined with a doubly serrate margin and a somewhat asymmetrical base, and arranged alternately on the stem. The bark is grayish with vertical ridges and deep furrows. Small, reddish flowers produce clusters of fruits called samaras. These are small (.5 inch long), brown, roundish seeds surrounded by a thin, ovate, pale green membrane fringed with tiny hairs. The American Elm has suffered greatly from the fungal Dutch elm disease, causing the loss of many trees, including those planted ornamentally in parks and homesteads.

Siberian Elm, *Ulmus pumila*
Elm family (Ulmaceae)
Alternate name(s): Dwarf Elm, Asiatic Elm
Size: Up to 65' tall, diameter to 1.5'
Range/habitat: Disturbed areas, fields, vacant urban lots of midwestern United States

Description: The Siberian Elm is an introduced tree from Asia. It is a medium-size, hardy, deciduous broadleaf tree with an open crown and light gray brown, coarsely furrowed bark. Leaves are alternate on the branches, dark green, elliptical, about 2 inches long, with pointed tips and serrate margins. The flowers are greenish, in small clusters, and produce thin, disclike, one-seeded pods called samaras. These fruits dry and fall to the ground or are carried some distance by the wind. This elm was initially cultivated as a fast-growing windbreak or shade tree and is considered by some to be undesirable because of its invasive nature and susceptibility to disease.

Southern Catalpa, *Catalpa Bigoniodes*
Trumpet-creeper family (Bigoniaceae)
Alternate name(s): Indian Bean Tree, Cigartree
Size: Up to 60' tall, diameter to 3'
Range/habitat: Streamsides, open bottomlands of southern Gulf states

Description: The Southern Catalpa is a medium-size, deciduous broadleaf tree with a short, thick trunk; spreading branches; and a low, broad, irregularly rounded crown. The leaves are cordate (heart-shaped), about 8 inches long, with pointed tips and smooth margins. They are bright green above, paler below, and arranged opposite on the branches or in whorls of three, supported by long leafstalks. They emit a foul odor when crushed. The bark is light brown to grayish brown, becoming shallowly fissured into narrow ridges and plates with age. The flowers, borne in tight, erect clusters, are bell-shaped, about 2 inches across, with asymmetrical, frilled, petal lobes. They are white with yellow and purple markings in the center. The fruit is a thin, long (to 24 inches), rounded capsule containing multiple winged seeds. The Southern Catalpa is popular as an ornamental or shade tree, and very similar to the Northern Catalpa of the Ohio and upper Mississippi River basins.

Sweetgum, *Liquidambar styraciflua*
Sweetgum family (Altingiaceae)
Alternate name(s): Redgum, Alligator-wood
Size: Up to 120' tall, diameter to 4'
Range/habitat: Wet lowland regions or higher slopes with moist soils throughout southeastern United States

Description: The Sweetgum is a common, deciduous broadleaf tree with dense foliage, a straight trunk, and broadly conical crown. The leaves are lustrous, loosely star shaped, about 6 inches long, with five (sometimes seven) pointed lobes and serrate margins. They are dark green above, paler below, have long, thin stalks, and grow alternately on branches. The foliage becomes brilliant orange, red, and purple in the autumn. The bark is brownish gray with thin, vertical ridges and furrows, and smaller branches are lined with strange, winglike, corky growths. The fruit is a globular cluster of spiky capsules, about 1.5 inches wide, growing on thin stalks. It begins green but turns brown and sometimes remains on the tree well into winter. The Sweetgum is named for the sweet sap of the inner bark. It is a popular ornamental and shade tree.

Index

About the Author/Illustrator

Todd Telander is a naturalist/illustrator/artist living in Walla Walla, Washington. He has studied and illustrated wildlife since 1989, while living in California, Colorado, New Mexico, and Washington. He graduated from the University of California at Santa Cruz with degrees in biology, environmental studies, and scientific illustration and has since illustrated numerous books and other publications, including FalconGuides' Scats and Tracks series. His wife, Kirsten Telander, is a writer, and he has two sons, Miles and Oliver. His work can be viewed online at toddtelander.com.